Alfred's Premier Piano Course

Dennis Alexander • Gayle Kowalchyk • E. L. Lancaster • Victor ... *Mier*

Edited by Morton Manus

Cover Design by Ted Engelbart
Interior Design by Tom Gerou
Illustrations by Jimmy Holder
Music Engraving by Linda Lusk

Contents

Alfred

Alfred Music Publishing Co., Inc.
P.O. Box 10003
Van Nuys, CA 91410-0003
alfred.com

ISBN-10: 0-7390-5935-1
ISBN-13: 978-0-7390-5935-7

A Note to Teachers

The art of playing the piano requires three things; knowledge, musical feeling, and the physical skills to perform what is artistically intended, also known as technique. The development of technique is essential to future success at the piano. Developing technique is a result of first understanding, then practicing the correct physical movements many times.

The technical tools and artistic skills learned in *Alfred's Premier Piano Course, Technique Books 1A, 1B and 2A*, are enhanced and expanded in *Technique Book 2B*. Each page in the Technique Book correlates with a specific page in the Lesson Book. When the Lesson, Theory, Performance and Technique books are used together, they offer a fully-integrated and unparalleled comprehensive approach to piano instruction.

In Technique Book 2B, students encounter technical skills in four areas, similar to 1A, 1B and 2A:

- Playing Naturally
- Moving Freely
- Playing Beautifully
- Playing Artistically

The technical goals in *Technique Book 2B* are accomplished through five types of activities:

Technique Tools from Books 1A, 1B and 2A* are reviewed and new technical goals for this level are clearly presented through appealing and descriptive exercises:

1. *Three-Note Slurs (p. 7)*
2. *Preparing Quickly for Hand Crossings (p. 11)*
3. *Feel the Downbeat (pp. 14–15)*
4. *Finger Stretches (p. 18)*
5. *Legato Pedal (p. 20)*
6. *Finger 1 under Finger 3 (p. 26)*
7. *Finger 3 over Finger 1 (p. 27)*

These Technique Tools should always be introduced to the student during the lesson.

Hands-Together Workshops focus on developing the skills necessary for coordinating hands-together playing.

Patterned Exercises provide students with the necessary repetitions to make the technique feel natural. Memorization, although optional, is suggested.

Artistic Etudes showcase a student's technique in an artistic musical setting.

Masterwork Etudes, written by important composers and teachers from the past, provide training to play standard masterworks. Many of them also reinforce *Technique Tools* and *Hands-Together Workshops*.

The overall goal of the Technique Books in *Alfred's Premier Piano Course* is to develop the physical skills needed to play artistically, expressively and effortlessly.

* See Technique Books 1A, 1B and 2A for descriptions of Technique Tools reviewed in this book.

Technique Tools Review

Demonstrate the following Technique Tools introduced in *Technique 2A*.

Seamless Melodies

Technique Tip: Match the sounds as the melody passes between the hands.

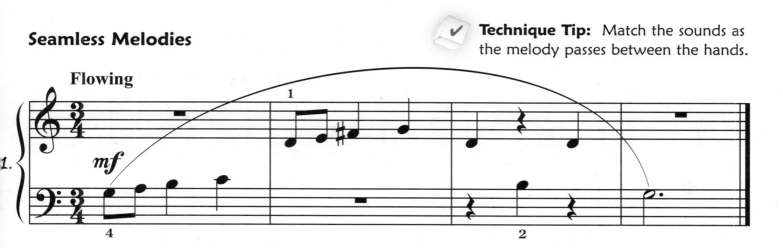

Dynamic Shaping

Technique Tip: Gradually *increase* the weight for each *crescendo* (⟨). Gradually *decrease* the weight for each *diminuendo* (⟩).

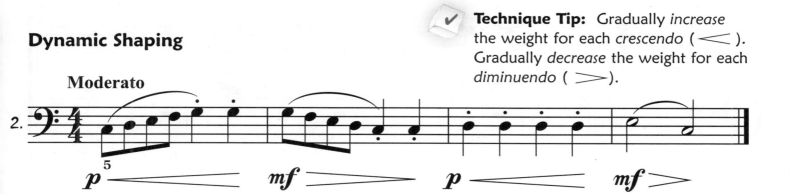

Crossing over the Thumb

Technique Tip: Play on the side tip of the thumb as you cross over with finger 2.

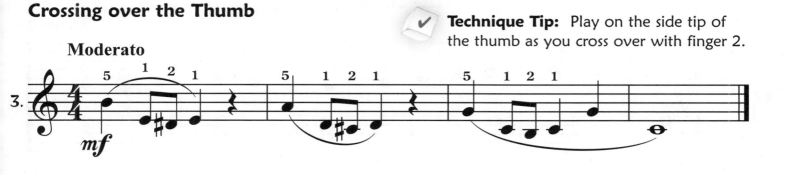

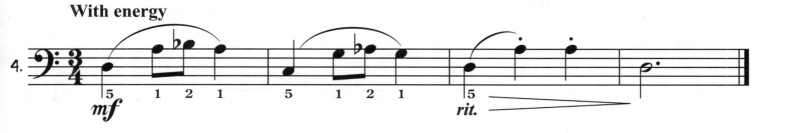

Technique Tools Review

Demonstrate the following Technique Tools introduced in *Technique 2A*.

Two-Note Slurs

✔ **Technique Tip:** Drop with *arm weight* onto the first note. Use a *rising wrist* as you play the second note.

Solid-Sounding Chords

✔ **Technique Tip:** Using *arm weight*, play each key so it touches the bottom of the key bed.

Play again in C major.

Balance Between RH Melody and Accompaniment

✔ **Technique Tip:** Listen carefully so that the melody sings out over the other notes.

Ode to Joy

Ludwig van Beethoven (1770–1827)
(adapted)

Play again in G major.

Damper Pedal Footwork

✔ **Technique Tip:** Lift the pedal and hand at the same time.

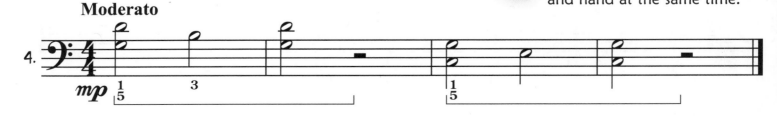

Masterwork Etude 1

Counterpoint

Counterpoint refers to a style of music that includes two or more melodies played together. In *Dialogue*, the LH melody begins a measure later than the RH melody.

Practice each hand separately before playing hands together.

Dialogue
(First Term at the Piano)

Béla Bartók
(1881–1945)

6

Falling Snowflakes
(Moving Freely)

 Technique Tip: *Move freely* using a gentle, *rising wrist* as you change positions.

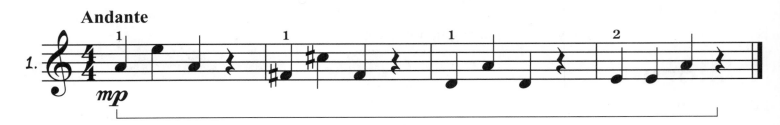

Technique Challenge: Play Nos. 1 and 2 hands together.

More or Less
(Dynamic Shaping)

 Technique Tip: Gradually increase the *finger* and *arm weight* for each *crescendo*; gradually decrease for each *diminuendo*.

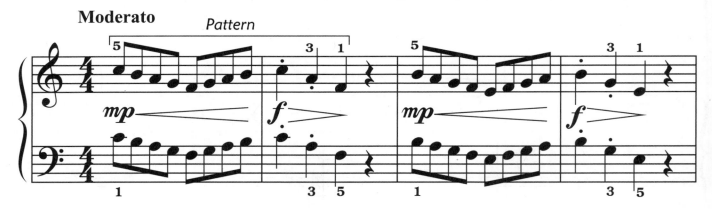

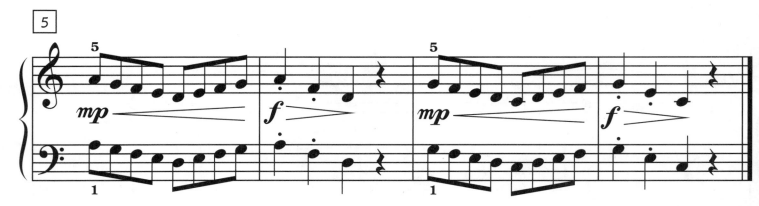

Technique Tool 1

Three-Note Slurs

A phrase consisting of three notes connected by a slur is called a *three-note slur*.
The first note is usually emphasized more than the other two notes.

On the closed keyboard cover, play *Three Up* and *Three Down*.

- Use *arm weight* and drop onto the first note.
- Gradually transfer the weight to the second and third notes.
- Use a *rising wrist* as you play the third note.
- After the third note, let the wrist lead the hand gently up from the keyboard.

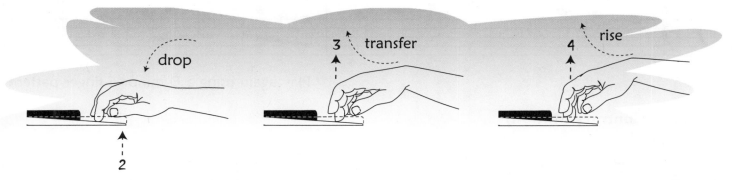

Three Up

✔ **Technique Tip:** On the *first* note, listen for a full, rich tone. On the *second* and *third* notes, listen for softer, lighter tones.

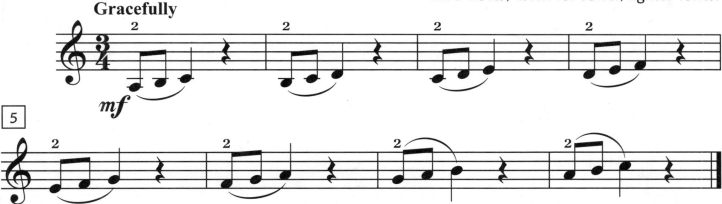

Play one octave *lower* with the LH, beginning each measure with finger 4.

Three Down

Play one octave *lower* with the LH, beginning each measure with finger 2.

Hands-Together Workshop 1   A and D Minor 5-Finger Patterns

The A and D minor 5-finger patterns are played on white keys only.
First practice slowly, then gradually increase the tempo.

A Minor (Parallel Motion)

 Technique Tip: Play with a rounded hand position and firm fingertips.

Play again using a D minor 5-finger pattern.

D Minor (Contrary Motion)

Play again using an A minor 5-finger pattern.

Side by Side

Ferdinand Beyer (1803–1863)
Op. 101, No. 44B
(adapted)

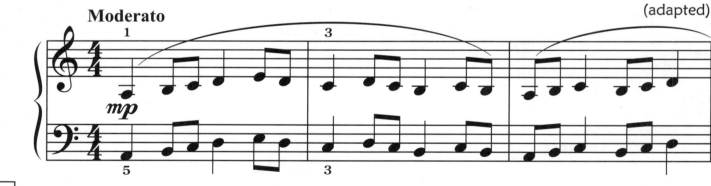

Play again using a D minor 5-finger pattern.

Hands-Together Workshop 2   C and G Minor 5-Finger Patterns

The C and G minor 5-finger patterns are played with four white keys and one black key in the middle (3rd finger). First practice slowly, then gradually increase the tempo.

C Minor (Parallel Motion)

Play again using a G minor 5-finger pattern.

G Minor (Contrary Motion)

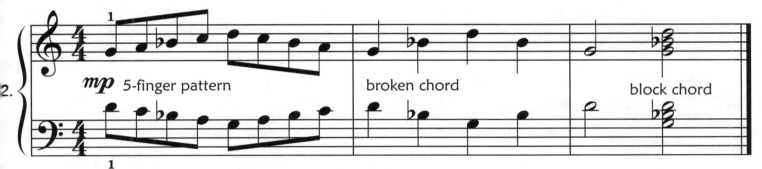

Play again using a C minor 5-finger pattern.

Parallel Motion Workout

Hands-Together Workshop 3 ## Major and Minor 5-Finger Patterns

First practice each example slowly; then gradually increase the tempo.

Parallel Motion Workout

Play again using a G 5-finger pattern.

Contrary Motion Workout

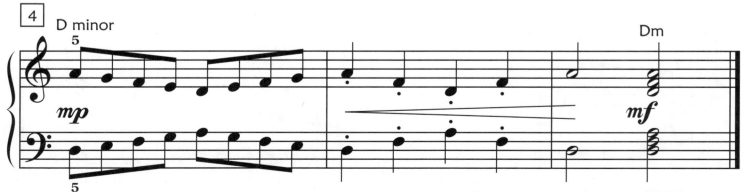

Play again using an A 5-finger pattern.

Technique Tool 2
Preparing Quickly for Hand Crossings

When one hand crosses over another, move "the crossing hand"
as soon as possible to its new location. Waiting too long to cross
will result in an uneven tempo.

Smooth Moves

 Technique Tip: Match the sounds as the notes
pass smoothly from hand to hand.

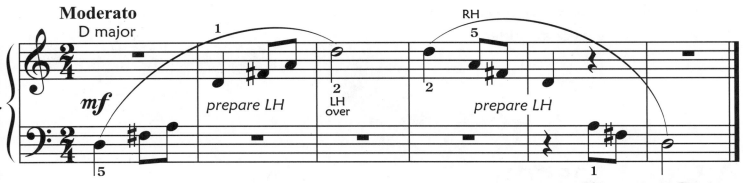

Play again in D minor.

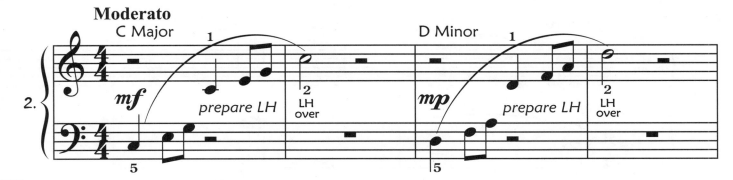

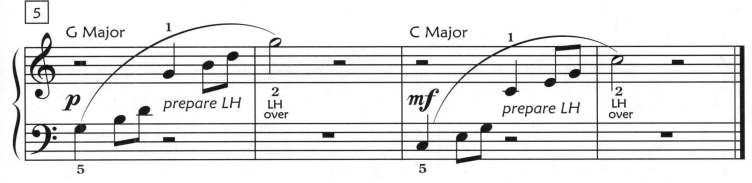

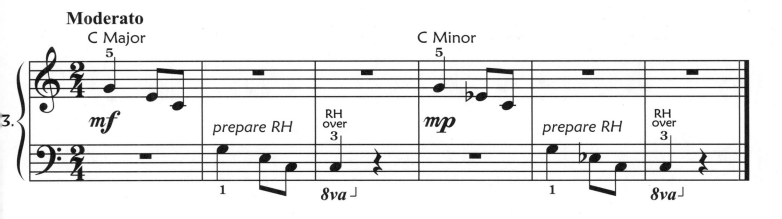

Artistic Etude 1

Playing with Continuity

Playing with continuity (no stops) requires special practice.

- In measures 17–24, circle the fingering where either hand *moves to a new location on the keyboard.*

- Now slowly play an outline version of these measures. To do this, play *only* the first circled note(s) when the hand moves to a new position.

- Gradually play faster using outline practice.

- Play the entire piece as written.

A Quiet Lagoon

✔ **Technique Tip:** *Prepare quickly* for the left-hand crossings.

Lesson Book: pages 16–17

Technique Tool 3

Feel the LH Downbeat

The first beat of each measure in $\frac{3}{4}$ and $\frac{4}{4}$ time is usually played with a slight emphasis. This is the *downbeat*. Other beats in the measure are usually played lightly.

On the closed keyboard cover, "play" the following rhythms with the correct hands.

- Use *more arm weight* for the downbeat (beat 1).

- Use *less arm weight* for other beats in the measure.

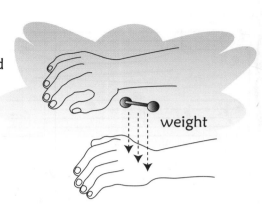

weight

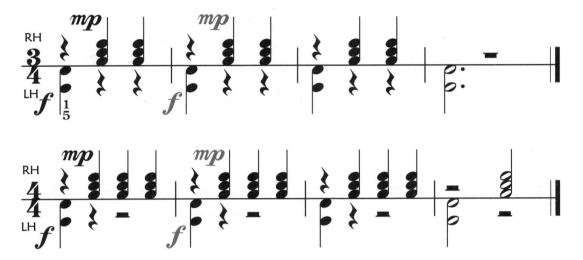

Feeling LH Downbeats

Technique Tip: Use *arm weight* and *strong fingertips* to get a full sound on beat 1. Play the RH with less weight and stay close to the keys.

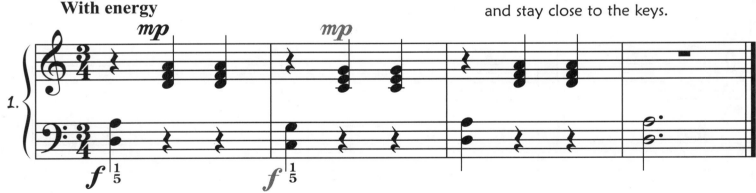

With energy

1.

Moderato

2.

Feel the RH Downbeat

On the closed keyboard cover, "play" the
following rhythms with the correct hands.

- Use *more arm weight* for beat 1.
- Use *less arm weight* for other beats in the measure.

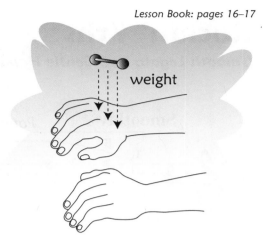
weight

Feeling RH Downbeats

✔ **Technique Tip:** Use *arm weight* and
strong fingertips to get a full sound on
beat 1. Play the LH with less weight
and stay close to the keys.

With energy

1.

Moderately

2.

Lesson Book: page 18

Rockin' 7ths
(Smooth Legato and Gentle Hand Rock)

 Technique Tip: Use a *gentle hand rock* on all melodic 7ths; use *arm weight* on all harmonic 7ths.

Play again, beginning on the C above Middle C.

Play again, beginning on the D above Middle C.

Creepy Crawlers on 6ths and 7ths

Keep your eyes on the music as you "crawl" up and down the keyboard
with 6ths and 7ths. As a challenge, play with your eyes closed!

Play with the LH one octave *lower*
beginning with finger 5.

Sixths and Sevenths

 Technique Tip: Play the second note of
each *two-note slur* softer than the first note.

18

Technique Tool 4

Finger Stretches

As you become more skilled at playing, your fingers will often stretch up or down from or within a 5-finger pattern.

- On the closed keyboard cover, "play" the LH part for the music below. Extend the fingers by stretching gently between fingers 3 and 1.

- Now "play" the RH part. Extend the fingers by stretching gently between fingers 1 and 2.

- Finally, "play" hands together.

✔ **Technique Tip:** Play with an even tone throughout.

Stretchin' with Hanon

Charles-Louis Hanon (1819–1900)
Op. 100, No. 8
(adapted)

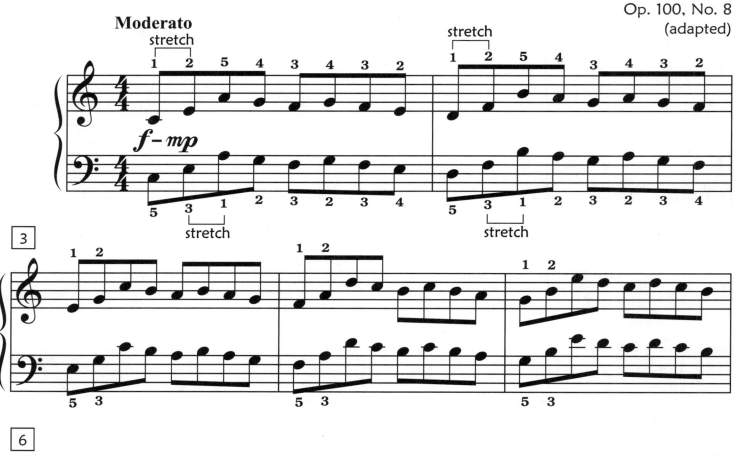

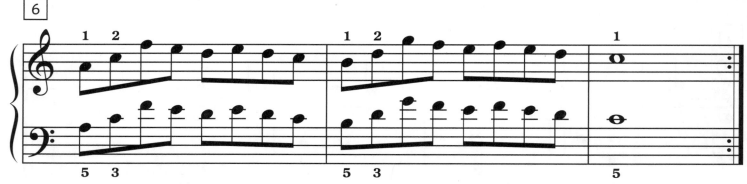

Masterwork Etude 2

Counterpoint

Practice each hand separately before
playing hands together.

Technique Tip: Emphasize the entrance
of the melody in each hand by using
more *arm weight* to *feel the downbeat.*

Weaving Melodies

Ferdinand Beyer (1803–1863)
Op. 101, No. 60

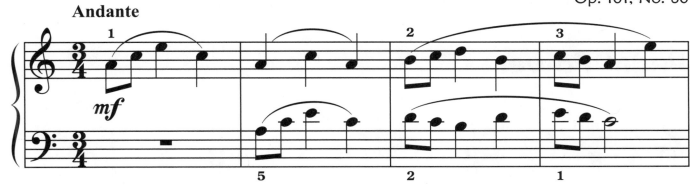

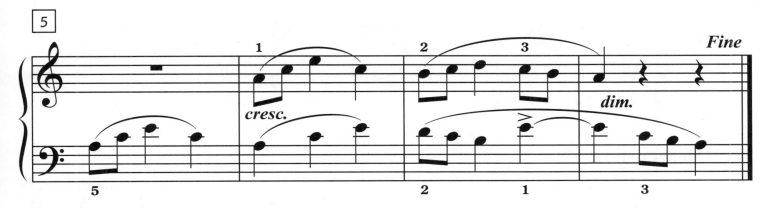

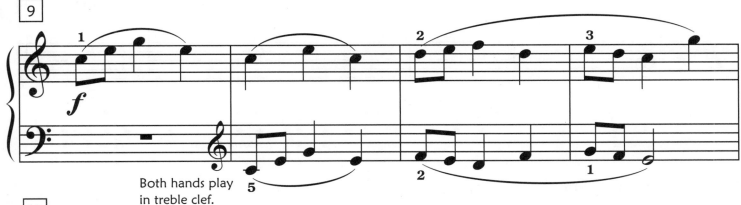

Both hands play
in treble clef.

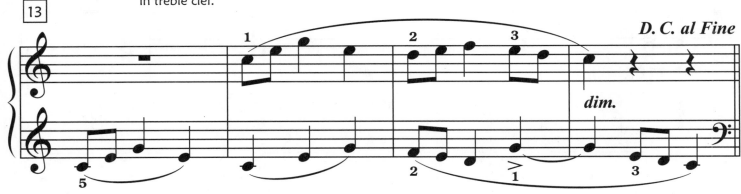

Technique Tool 5

Legato Pedal

The damper pedal helps create *legato* sounds when your fingers alone cannot.

Raise the damper pedal at the exact moment that you play the notes above the up-down (‿⋏) pedal sign. Then quietly and quickly press it down again.

- First play *Pedal Power 1* while holding the damper pedal down throughout.
  What happens to the sounds?
- Now play *Pedal Power 1*, 2, and 3, making sure to lift the pedal at the exact moment each new chord is played. Practice saying "up" exactly when the pedal lifts.

Pedal Power

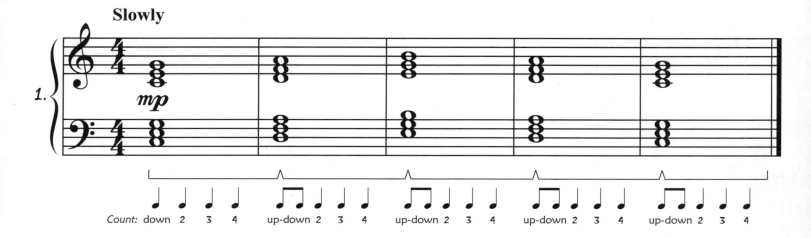

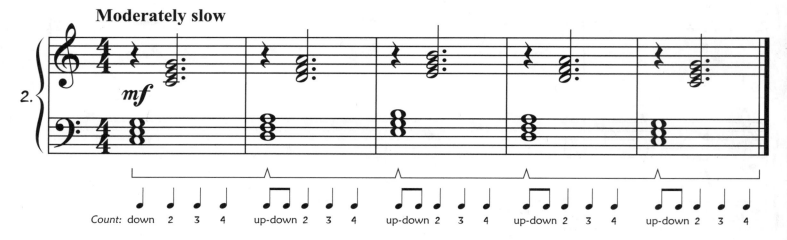

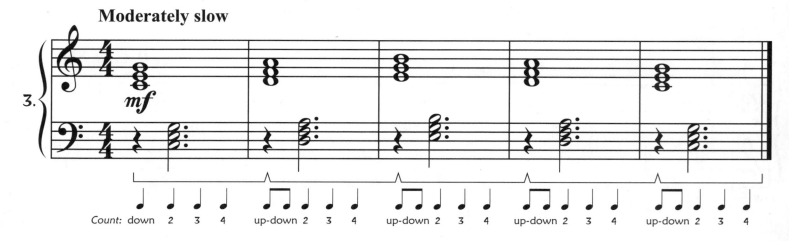

Legato Pedal

In each example, listen for a smooth and connected pedal.

Simple Footwork

(Feel the Downbeat)

 Technique Tip: Use less weight for the notes on beats 2 and 3. Listen for a softer sound.

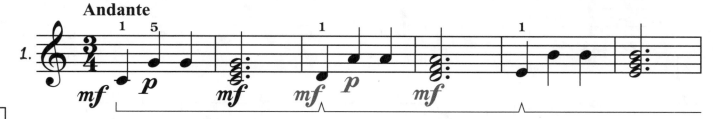

Top Note Leads

 Technique Tip: Play with a lighter touch on beat 3 of each measure.

Lesson Book: page 24

Rockin' Octaves
(Gentle Hand Rock)

Students with small hands should lift off the lower note of the octave to play the higher note.

 Technique Tip: When playing octaves, relax your arms and shoulders. You can *stretch* more easily that way.

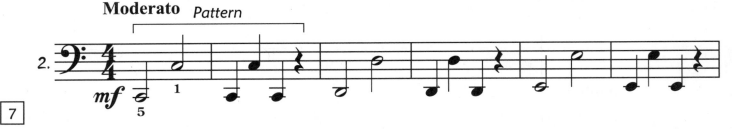

Climbing the Rock Wall
(Legato Pedal)

 Technique Tip: Lift the pedal exactly when marked and then quickly press it down again.

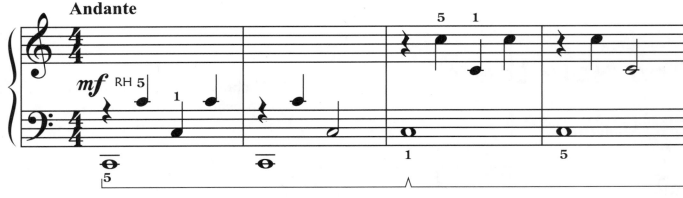

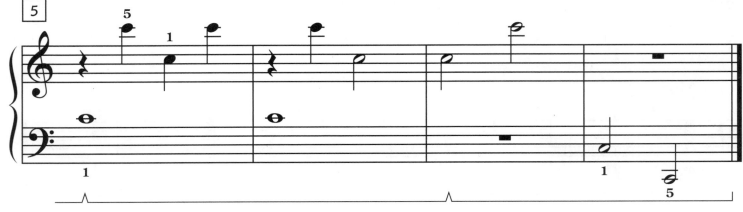

Creepy Crawlers on 7ths and Octaves

Keep your eyes on the music as you "crawl" up and down the keyboard
with 7ths and octaves. As a challenge, play with your eyes closed!

mf

Play with the LH one octave *lower*
beginning with finger 5.

Finger GPS

✓ **Technique Tip:** Play the second note of
each *two-note slur* softer than the first note
by lifting gently with a rising wrist.

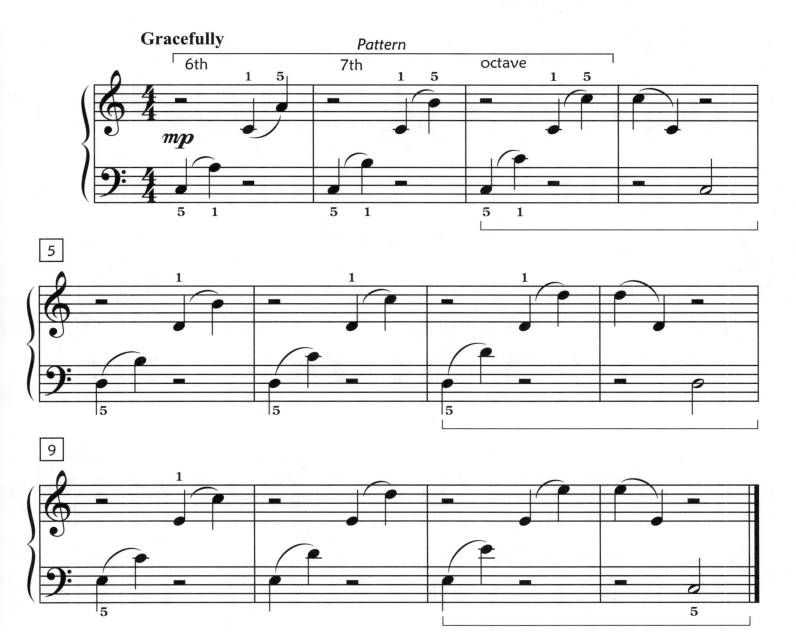

Artistic Etude 2

Playing with a Dramatic Sound

Dramatic pieces often have:

- A *broad range of dynamics*—change your arm weight to play from soft to loud.

- A *dramatic tempo marking*—follow it carefully, and never play faster.

- A *descriptive title*—keep the title and/or its story in your mind as you play. Have fun as you express the drama!

Royal Wedding

✔ **Technique Tip:** Use *arm weight* to create a full sound and *feel the downbeat* of each measure.

Lesson Book: pages 28–29

Technique Tool 6

Finger 1 under Finger 3 (Preparation for Scales)

● On the closed keyboard cover, "play" *One Under Three* with the correct fingers.

● Keep the fingertip and thumb tip close together as you "play."

Repeat 3 times each day.

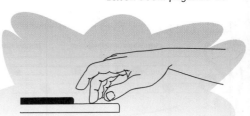

One Under Three

✔ **Technique Tip:** Listen for a smooth connection as finger 1 passes *under* finger 3.

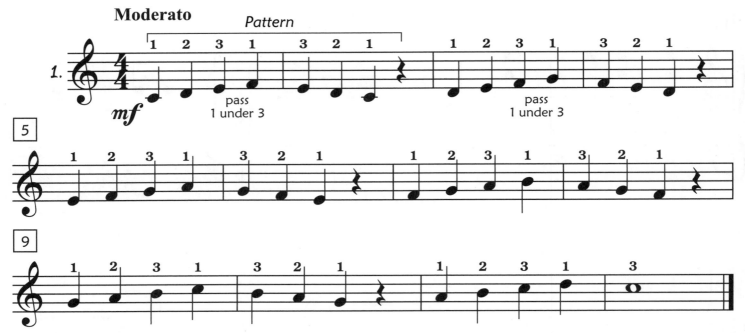

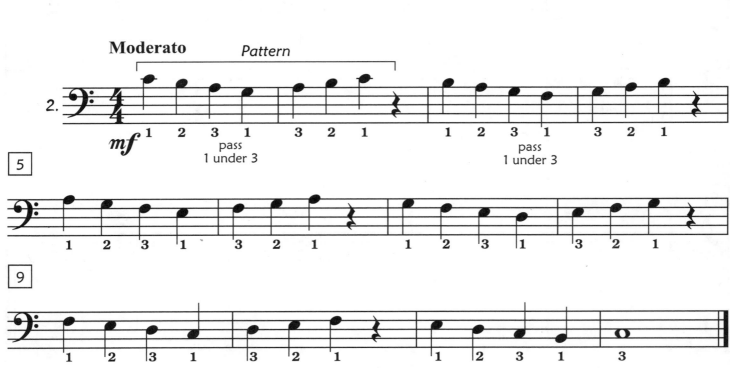

Technique Challege: Play Nos. 1 and 2 hands together. Both thumbs start on Middle C.

Technique Tool 7

Finger 3 over Finger 1 (Preparation for Scales)

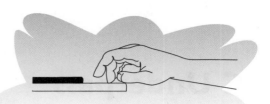

- On the closed keyboard cover, "play" *Three Over One* with the correct fingers.

- Keep the fingertip and thumb tip close together as you "play."

Repeat 3 times each day.

Three Over One

✔ **Technique Tip:** Listen for a smooth connection as finger 3 crosses *over* finger 1.

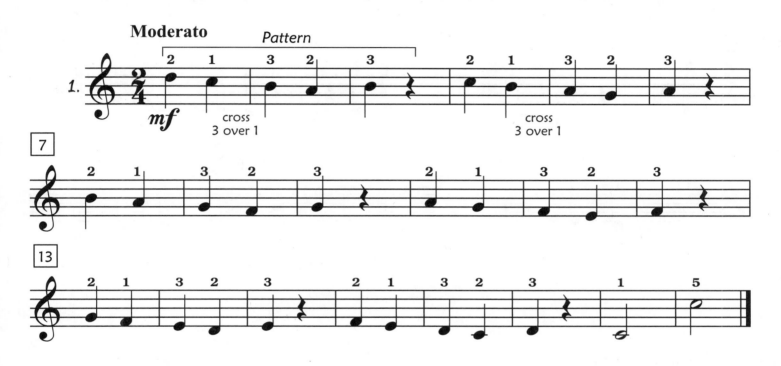

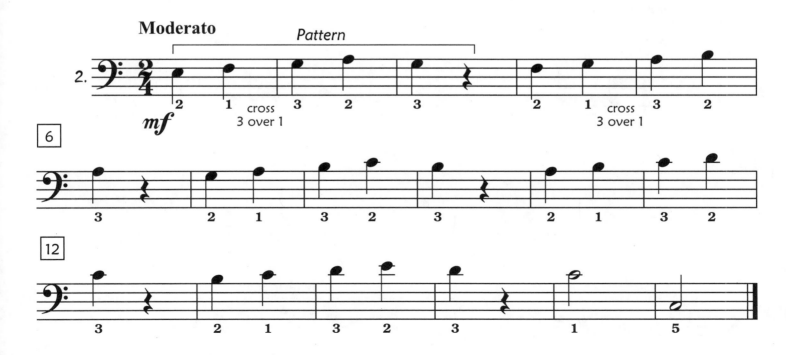

Lesson Book: page 30

C Major Scale Crossings

C Underpass
(Finger 1 under Finger 3)

✔ **Technique Tip:** Keep the wrist level with no bounces when finger 1 passes under finger 3.

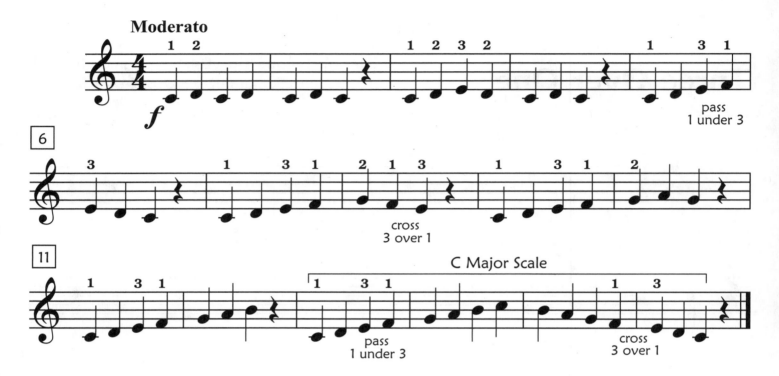

C Overpass
(Finger 3 over Finger 1)

✔ **Technique Tip:** Keep the wrist level with no bounces when finger 3 crosses over finger 1.

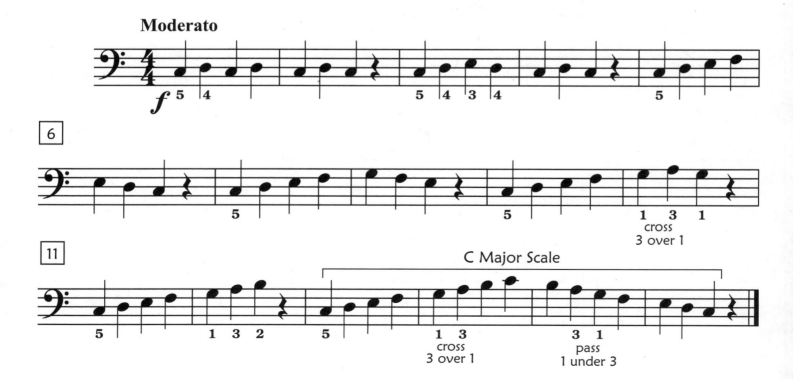

G Major Scale Crossings

G Underpass
(Finger 1 under Finger 3)

 Technique Tip: Keep the wrist level with no bounces when finger 1 passes under finger 3.

G Overpass
(Finger 3 over Finger 1)

 Technique Tip: Keep the wrist level with no bounces when finger 3 crosses over finger 1.

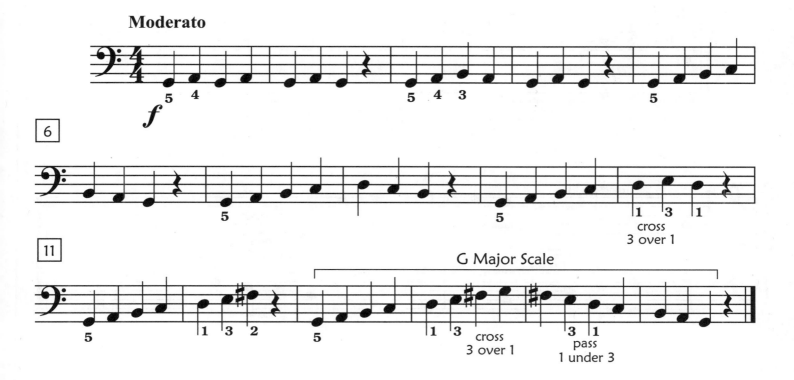

Hands-Together Workshop 4   Major Scales in Contrary Motion

Going My Own Way

Technique Tip: Listen to all the notes played by the thumb. They should match the sound of the surrounding notes and should not sound louder or softer.

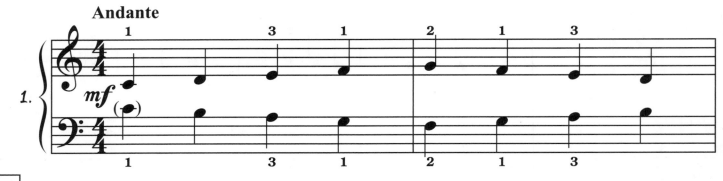

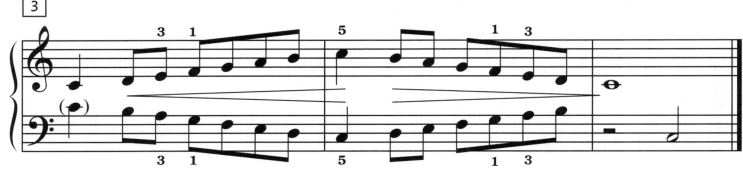

Technique Tip: In contrary motion, the same numbered fingers of each hand play at the same time.

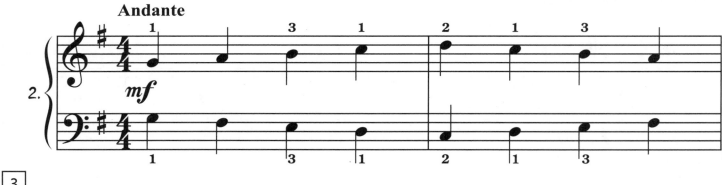

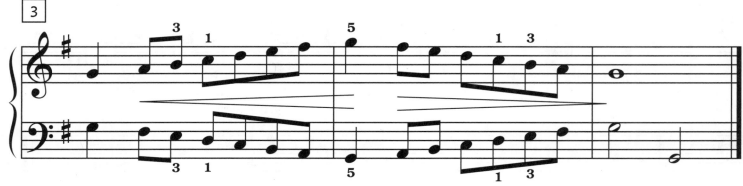

Closing the Gap
(Finger Stretches)

Name each melodic interval.

Technique Tip: Use a *gentle hand rock* to play each melodic interval.

Transpose to G major.

The Perfect Waltz
(Feel the Downbeat)

Technique Tip: Say "strong, light, light" as you play.

Harmonic Intervals

Practice each hand separately before playing hands together. Name each harmonic interval.

The I and V⁷ Chords in C
(Solid-Sounding Chords)

✔ **Technique Tip:** Using *arm weight*, feel your fingers touch firmly and evenly for each chord change.

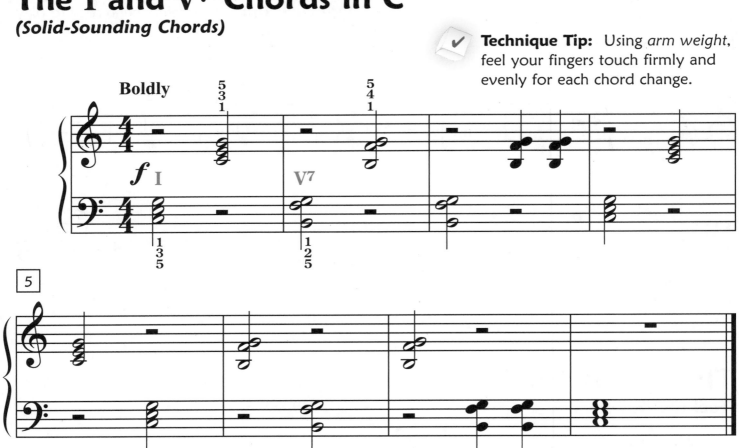

Melody and Chord Balance

✔ **Technique Tip:** Create a perfect balance by playing the melody slightly louder than the chords.

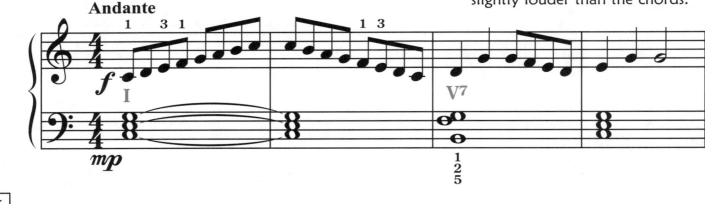

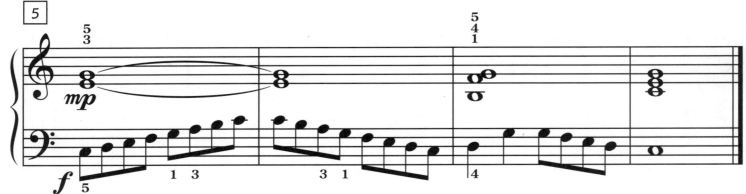

The I and V⁷ Chords in G
(Solid-Sounding Chords)

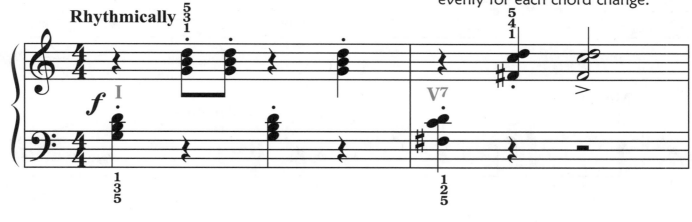

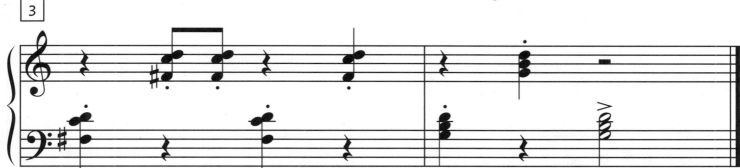

Play again in the key of C.

Melody and Chord Balance

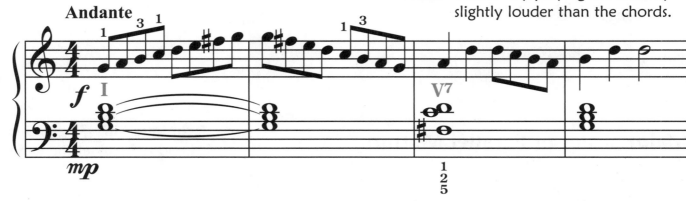

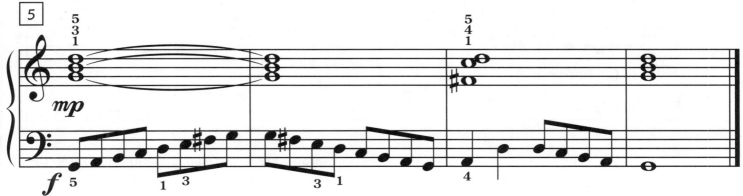

RH Finger Twisters

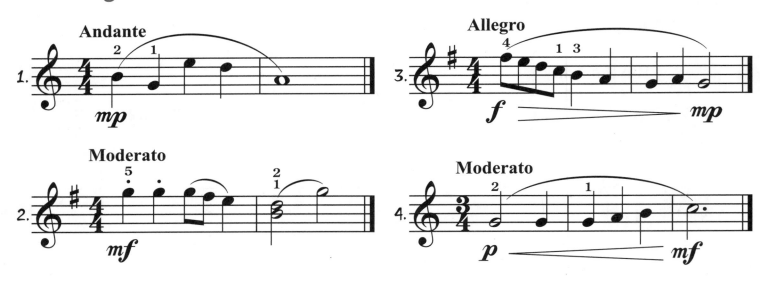

LH Finger Twisters

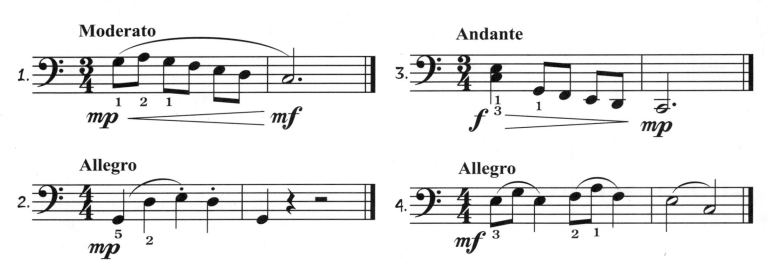

Major Scales in Parallel Motion

✓ **Technique Tip:** Fingers 3 in the LH and RH play at the same time.

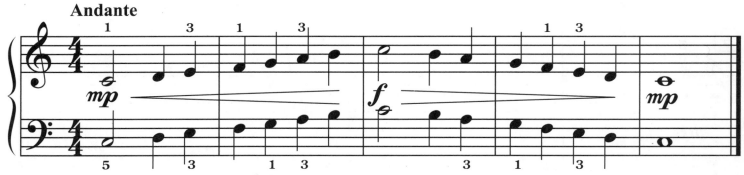

Play the G major scale in parallel motion hands together.

Technique Tip: Keep your arm and hand relaxed when playing the *finger stretches* in *Hanon Goes Jazzy.*

Hanon Goes Jazzy
(Finger Stretches)

Charles-Louis Hanon (1819–1900)
Op. 100, No. 10
(adapted)

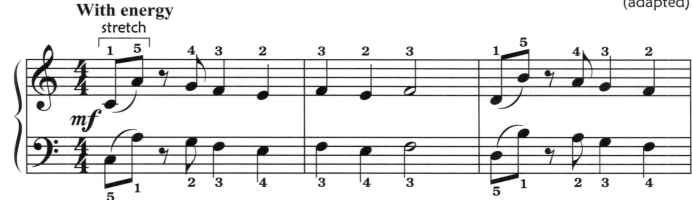

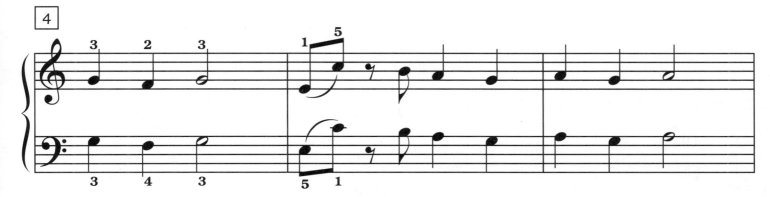

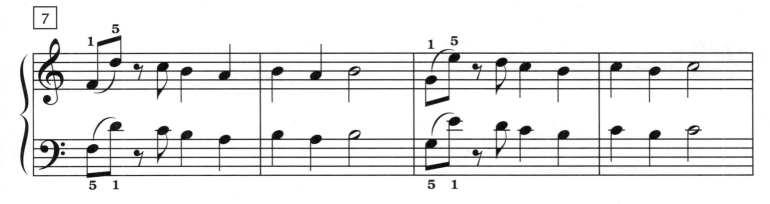

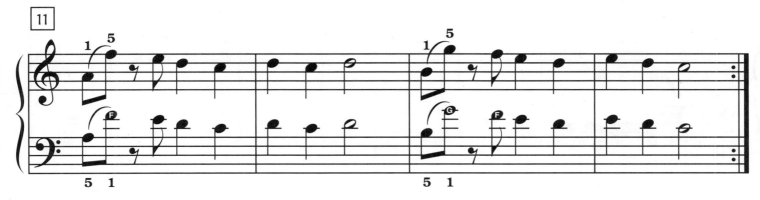

Dotted Quarter Note Technique

(Finger 1 under Finger 3)

1.

Moderato

mf

Play again using a C major scale.

(Finger 3 over Finger 1)

2.

Moderato

mf

Play again using a C major scale.

(Preparing Quickly for Hand Crossings)

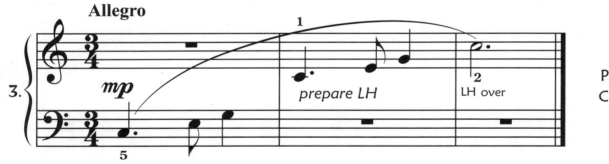

3.

Allegro

mp

prepare LH

LH over

Play again using a
C minor arpeggio.

(Solid-Sounding Chords)

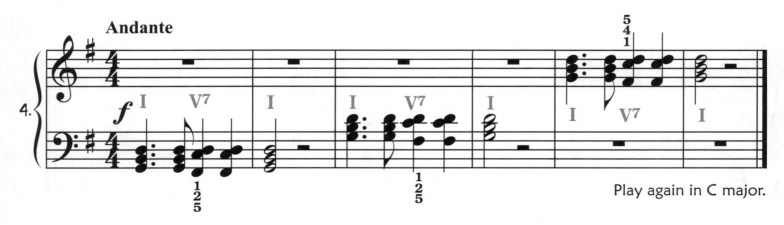

4.

Andante

f I V7 I I V7 I I V7 I

Play again in C major.

Masterwork Etude 3

Gentle Hand Rock

Village Dance

> ✔ **Technique Tip:** Keep your wrists and
> arms level as you *gently rock* from
> finger to finger in *Village Dance*.

Béla Bartók (1881–1945)

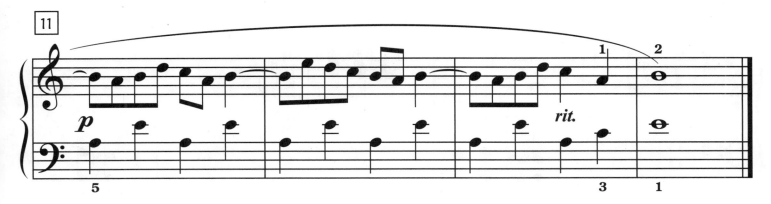

Artistic Etude 3

Rhythm and Musical Mood

Many piano pieces have a strong rhythmic "feel" that projects the musical mood.
To convey the rhythmic "feel" of measures 1–12, follow these steps:

- On the closed keyboard cover, tap the rhythm hands separately, then hands together.

- On the open keyboard, play very slowly at first. When you can play all the rhythms 100% accurately with no pauses, begin playing at a slightly faster tempo (speed).

- Finally, play up to tempo (but no faster than the tempo marking) while projecting the mood of the music.

Cool Mood

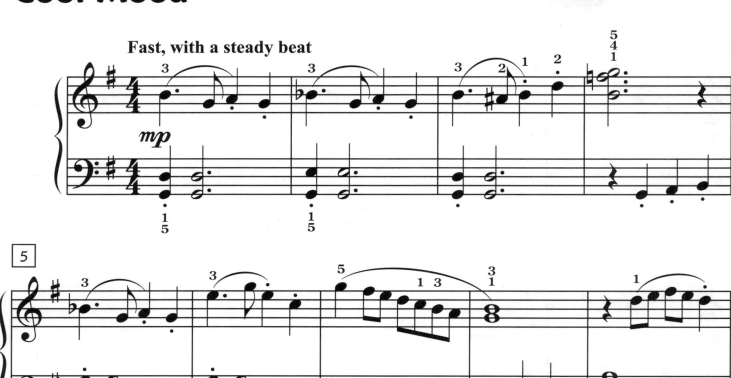

Technique Tools Review

Circle the Technique Tool needed to play each example.
Then play, using that Technique Tool.

1. Preparing Quickly
for Hand Crossings
or
Feel the Downbeat
(circle one)

2. Preparing Quickly
for Hand Crossings
or
Three-Note Slurs
(circle one)

3. Finger Stretches
or
Finger 1 under Finger 3
(circle one)

4. Finger 3 over Finger 1
or
Finger Stretches
(circle one)

5. Three-Note Slurs
or
Feel the Downbeat
(circle one)